LEVEL
3

D0546175

Elephants

Laura Marsh

NATIONAL
GEOGRAPHIC

For Jackie, Billy, Jane and Lilly — L.F.M.

Copyright © 2010, 2014 National Geographic Society

Published by the National Geographic Society, Washington, D.C. 20036

Library of Congress Cataloging-in-Publication Data
Marsh, Laura F.
Great migrations. Elephants / by Laura Marsh.
p. cm.
Includes index.
ISBN 978-1-4263-0743-0 (pbk. : alk. paper) -- ISBN 978-1-4263-0744-7 (library binding : alk. paper)
1. African elephant--Migration--Juvenile literature. I. Title.
QL737.P98M3697 2010
599.67'41568--dc22
2010017961

UK ISBN: 978-1-4263-1803-0

Abbreviation Key: GET = Getty Images; IS = iStockphoto.com; NGS = NationalGeographicStock.com; NGT = National Geographic Television; SS = Shutterstock.com

Elephants marching throughout, Carlton W... ...S; Weighty Word
throughout: Jason Prince/ SS; Cover, Carlton ... ...tom), NGT; 5 (top),
John Eastcott and Yva Momatiuk/ NGS; 6 (ce... ...na Andrushko/ SS;
11 (right), Jodi Cobb/ NGS;11 (top), Michael G... ...tre), Carlton Ward
Jr; 14, Artem Efimov/SS; 15, Carlton Ward Jr; 16... ...rd Jr; 17 (bottom),
Carlton Ward Jr; 18, Jim Kruger/ IS; 19 (top), ...rski/ Corbis; 22-23
(centre), Carlton Ward Jr; 24 (bottom centre), ..., Michael Nichols/
NGS; 27, Martin Harvey/ Gallo Images/ Corbi... ...el Nichols/ NGS; 32
(top left), Michael Nichols/ NGS; 32 (top righ... .../ NGS; 32 (bottom
left), Jodi Cobb/ NGS; 32 (bottom right), Java... ...Jr; 33 (centre left),
Carlton Ward Jr; 33 (centre right), Michael Ni... ...5-37, Carlton Ward
Jr; 37, Gerry Ellis/ Minden Pictures/ NGS; 38, ...riy Korchagin/ IS;
43 (bottom centre), Tim Fitzharris/ Minden P... ...e Quintos/ NGS;46
(centre left), Micheal Nichols/ NGS; 46 (top ri... ...right), Jodi Cobb/
NGS; 46 (bottom right), Carlton Ward Jr; 47 (... ...e left), Gerry Ellis/
Minden Pictures/ NGS; 47 (bottom left), Rich...

Printed in the United States of America
14/WOR/1

Table of Contents

On the Move

When animals travel from one region or habitat to another, it is called migration. Animals migrate in search of food or a mate. Migration helps animals survive on Earth.

Many animals migrate. The Mali elephant is one of them.

elephants

4

wildebeest

red crabs

Weighty Words

MIGRATION: Moving from one region or habitat to another for food or a mate

MATE: Either a male or female in a pair — most animals need a mate to have babies

What animal...

Can travel over 140km a day?

Has tusks used to dig for water and find food

Is the largest land animal on Earth?

An elephant!

Elephants live in Africa and Asia. This book is about the elephants that live on the southern border of the Sahara desert in Mali, West Africa.

How Do We Measure Up?

An African elephant is so big, it makes a tall man look small.

Everything African Elephant

HEIGHT:
2.4–4m tall

WEIGHT:
2,270–6,350kg

LIFE SPAN:
Up to 70 years

SIZE:
Largest land
animal on Earth

SKIN: Wrinkled and grey.
Elephants spray water and
dust over their skin to stay
cool in the hot sun.

FEET: Hooved, with
spongy pads that
absorb weight.

EARS: Keep elephants cool by releasing heat.

TUSKS: Used to dig for water and for roots to eat. They are also used to strip bark from trees for a tasty meal.

TRUNK: It's used for smelling, drinking, breathing, trumpeting and spraying water over the elephant's body. It has two fingerlike ends for grabbing.

Enormous Appetites

Elephants are herbivores. They eat only plants, such as roots, grasses, fruit and bark. Elephants need to eat a lot to fuel their massive bodies – up to 135kg per day. That's like eating 1,200 hamburgers!

The Mali elephants' habitat is the woodland area near watering holes.

Weighty Words

HERBIVORE: An animal that eats only plants

HABITAT: The place or environment where a plant or animal naturally lives

tree bark

papayas

grass

Sticking Together

Female elephants and young elephants form a group called a herd. Herds are led by an older female and usually have six to 20 elephants. But in some areas, much larger herds have been seen.

Females stay with the same herd their whole lives. But males only remain with the herd until they are 12 to 15 years old. Then they join a group of other males, called a bachelor herd, or live alone.

Male and female herds migrate separately.

Elephants Never Forget

Scientists think that elephants have good memories. Herd leaders remember where the best watering holes are, even if they have not been there in several years.

Weighty Word

HERD: A large group of wild animals

Tough Travel

Mali elephants migrate farther than any other elephants. Scientists estimate they travel between 450 and 700km. Travelling 700km is like walking from York to London and back every year!

weird but true

Elephants sleep standing up.

700km round trip

York

London

Elephant Mileage

Scientists are able to find out how far an elephant travels by attaching a GPS tracking collar around its neck. The elephant is given medicine to make it fall asleep so that the scientists can safely attach the collar. When the elephant wakes up, it joins the herd and goes on its way.

Full Circle

The Mali elephants start and end their journey at Lake Banzena. It contains the only year-round watering hole in the area. All other watering holes disappear during the dry season.

The elephants spend the dry season at Lake Banzena. But by April and May there is little food at Banzena because elephants and other animals have eaten it. It is time to move on.

When the rainy season begins, the elephants travel south. The rain renews old watering holes and allows nutritious new food to grow elsewhere.

Weighty Word

INSTINCT: Behaviour that animals are born knowing how to do

Perfect Timing

The elephants begin their migration south as soon as the first rain begins. They know by instinct that it's time to migrate.

The elephants eat the plants around a small watering hole and then move on. They travel from watering hole to watering hole for many months. Their route makes a big circle.

By November, the rains stop and it's time to return to Lake Banzena, where they spend another dry season. But the elephants must hurry before the watering holes along the way dry up. They can't live without water.

Baby Elephants

When baby elephants
are born, they
weigh about 90kg.
That's as much as
a large adult man.

Newborn elephants
are one metre – about
the height of a sofa.

Baby elephants are called calves. They drink their mother's milk until they are four or five years old. Calves might suck on their trunks for comfort, just like babies suck their thumbs.

Weighty Word

CALF:
A baby elephant

25

Elephant Talk

weird but true

Elephants can make more than 25 separate sounds that mean different things.

Elephants use different parts of their bodies to gather and send information.

They use their mouths and trunks to grumble, growl and trumpet. This is how they talk to each other.

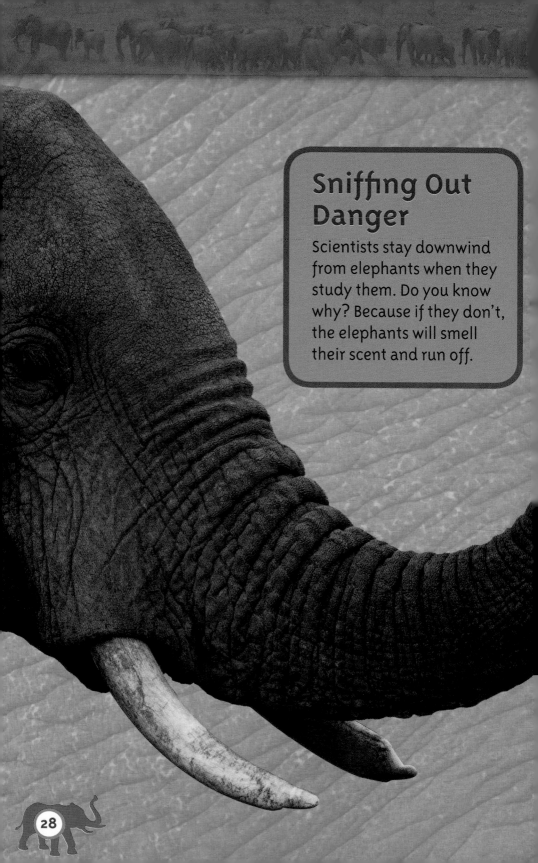

Sniffing Out Danger

Scientists stay downwind from elephants when they study them. Do you know why? Because if they don't, the elephants will smell their scent and run off.

Elephants use their trunks to smell if other animals are nearby. If they sense danger, they call to each other. Then the adults circle around the young elephants to protect them.

Elephants use
their feet
to feel sound
vibrations
through the
earth. Scientists
think they can
feel sounds such
as the movement
of other herds
occurring up to
30km away.

Elephants use their trunks to greet each other and show affection. Sometimes they hook their trunks together in a kind of elephant hug.

10 Cool Things About Elephants

1 Elephants can weigh as much as 7,000kg — more than two big jeeps.

2 Elephants don't sleep much. They need to spend a lot of time looking for food.

3 They make loud, low sounds that other elephants can hear up to 10km away.

4 Their ears give off heat to keep them cool in hot temperatures.

5 Mother elephants are pregnant for 22 months. That's almost two years!

6 Unlike human newborns, calves can stand within an hour of birth.

7 They can run as fast as 40km an hour and travel over 190km in one day.

8 Each elephant's ears are different. Scientists can tell individual elephants by their ear shapes and markings.

9 Elephants favour their right or left tusk — just like we favour our right or left hand.

10 A herd leader makes all decisions for the herd, such as where to go and when to stop, eat and drink.

Elephant Emergency

More than 1,000 elephants once roamed all across Mali. Now there are fewer than 400 elephants.

What happened to the Mali elephants?

34

An elephant's
tusks keep
growing
throughout
its adult life.

1,000 elephants

400 elephants

Now

Then

 = 100 elephants

35

Poachers killed many elephants in the 1970s and 1980s. They only wanted the elephants' tusks and sold them at high prices.

Although poaching is outlawed, it is still a problem today.

Weighty Word

POACHER: Someone who hunts animals illegally

weird but true

An elephant's trunk has about 100,000 different muscles, but no bones.

Elephant tusks are made of ivory, which has been used to make things like jewellery and piano keys.

Mali elephants are trying to survive in difficult conditions. There is less water and fewer plants than there used to be. One reason is because the Earth has become warmer. Higher temperatures are drying up water sources.

But people are making it harder for elephants, too. They are settling where elephants live and migrate. So there is less and less land for the elephants. Also, livestock owned by local people are eating plants and drinking water that elephants need, too.

Q Why was the elephant asked to leave the swimming pool?

A He couldn't hold up his trunks!

Weighty Word!

LIVESTOCK: Animals raised to sell or use

Helping Mali Elephants

Scientists are keeping track of the number of elephants so that if elephant numbers go down, they can find a solution before it's too late.

Scientists are also tagging elephants with special collars to track them. The collars show scientists exactly where the elephants travel. Then people can build roads and homes elsewhere. This will create safe migration paths for the elephants.

weird but true

An elephant's skin can be 2.5cm thick in some areas.

Water Heroes

In 1983, a huge drought dried up all water sources for the elephants. The Mali government brought water in big trucks. Many elephant lives were saved.

In May 2009, another drought occurred. A group called Save the Elephants built an emergency water tank. Unfortunately, these solutions are expensive. It is difficult to get and keep enough water for everyone in dry regions.

Weighty Word

DROUGHT: A long period with little or no rain

There is protected reserve land
where elephants can live.
But only a small part
of the elephants' range
is on this land. More
protected land is needed.

Local people in the Mali government want the elephants to survive. Mali children learn about the elephants in school. The more people know, the better we can help the elephants.

What You Can Do

To learn more about Mali elephants and their amazing migration, check out these organisations that help them.

Living With Elephants

http://www.livingwithelephants.org

National Geographic Society

http://kids.nationalgeographic.com/Animals/
CreatureFeature/African-elephant

Save the Elephants

http://www.savetheelephants.org

The WILD Foundation

http://www.wild.org/field-projects/
the-desert-elephants-of-mali

Glossary

MATE: Either a male or fema in a pair — most animals nee a mate to have babies

MIGRATION: Moving from one region or habitat to another for food or a mate

INSTINCT: Behaviour that animals are born knowing how to do

CALF: A baby elephant

POACHER: Someone who hunt animals illegally

BITAT: The place or vironment where a plant animal naturally lives

HERBIVORE: An animal that only eats plants

RD: A large group of wild animals

VESTOCK: Animals raised sell or use

DROUGHT: A long period with little or no rain

Index